T0365101

The Awakening

Ronnie V. Broadus

iUniverse®

THE AWAKENING

iUniverse books may be ordered through booksellers or by contacting:

iUniverse
1663 Liberty Drive
Bloomington, IN 47403
www.iuniverse.com
844-349-9409

ISBN: 978-1-4401-8843-5 (sc)
ISBN: 978-1-4401-8845-9 (hc)
ISBN: 978-1-4401-8844-2 (e)

Print information available on the last page.

iUniverse rev. date: 11/30/2021

I would like to dedicate this book to four people or groups of people. The first person is Mrs. Brendolyn Broadus, who is with the Lord now. She was not only my wife, but also my friend from 1984 to 2008, when she departed this journey to be with the Lord. I am keeping my promise to her—that I would tell the world about her and the life that we shared.

The second person or persons I dedicate this book to are all the physically challenged people of this world. I hope that my book will bring you much joy and happiness and the will to never, never give up. Your journeys have not ended, they have only begun.

Next, I dedicate this book to you, the reader. Wherever you are in this world, may you find the joy and happiness that I have found in my believing and thoughts that this journey is not over,it is only a beginning for you. I hope also that if you haven't yet, you will be awakened, and that you realize your true journey is in front of you.

Finally, I dedicate this book to God, his Son Jesus, and his blessed Holy Spirit, who have opened my eyes and ears and helped me to comprehend what it truly means to live in the Kingdom of God.

Introduction

I was between eight and ten years of age when I first became aware of God's presence in my life. There were four significant seasons of my life during which His presence or voice made a direct impact on me. Even though I did not know it at the time, I know it now. You see, dear reader, He has been very real to me ever since He has awakened me to the journey we call life.

The first significant event of my life in which I felt God's presence occurred when I was at my home church, 8th Street Baptist Church located in Temple, Texas. I was eight or nine years old. My usual routine on Sundays was to go to Sunday school, then to worship service. Afterward I would either go to the movies, when my mom had money, or watch the Dallas Cowboys play their weekly game.

This was simply a routine; I had no particular choice or opinion about my Sunday schedule. It was the law of our home, set down by my mom. I had been brought up in a Baptist home; all my family members were Baptist, including my cousins. Most of the town was Baptist, so there was no choice for me but to be a Baptist. I didn't understand this, for my oldest brother, Karl, only went to church on Easter. On Sundays, he was usually fishing at the local fishing hole, but me—I had to go to church.

Some of my classmates also went to the same church, and they often gave me a tough time because I was not baptized. How they knew this, I don't know. One Sunday, they were riding me again about it. How could I not even know what baptism was? They'd chide. What I had heard about it scared me to death. Who wanted to get drowned in a pool of water by a strange man you didn't even know!

My mom would often give me money for church, and I would go between Sunday school and worship services and buy candy. Whatever was left over was what the church got; usually it was a nickel or some pennies. One particular Sunday, I was sitting in my regular seat at the church, in the back row, eating my candy and not bothering anybody. That is when God came into my life.

I cannot remember exactly what happened to me, but I got up from my seat, walked through the church members and the deacons, sat myself down in the sinner's seat, and announced to the church that I wanted to get baptized. I had become a candidate for baptism, and it was not going to happen not next week or next month—it was going to happen that night.

Of course my mom, aunts, cousins, and other family members were all happy for me because this was the right thing to do, but I was scared to death. That night, I entered the baptismal pool. A large man wearing a black robe entered the baptismal pool, took me by my head, took me under water, and then brought me back up. I was submerged for only a short time, but to me, time stood still. Honestly, until this day, I often relive the experience. Was I traumatized or scarred? No, I was baptized.

When I was twenty-two years of age I experienced my second significant event involving God's presence. I had enlisted in the United States Navy. I was in my second year and had put in an application for officer's school. I had wanted to fly F-14 fighter planes and then go on to become a United States senator. I had big dreams.

But for now, I was working my shift as a communications supervisor. My commanding officer requested that I come to his office. I wondered what I had done and thought that maybe he was going to question me about the gambling I had been doing with other enlisted men, knowing that supervisors had no business gambling onboard ship. When I arrived at his office, he requested that I sit down. I knew that I was in big trouble. He began to speak, saying solemnly that I had to go home, that there had been a death in my family. I asked him who had died, and he said my sister.

Around this time, my mother was pregnant, and I figured that she had suffered a miscarriage. I collected my thoughts, took emergency leave, and got home on the first plane leaving San Diego. When I got to Temple, Texas, I took a walk to gather myself before going home and decided to go and see my best friend, Steve, and let him know that I was home.

We shared hellos, and then he said that he was sorry about my sister's death. I said to him that it was okay, my mom had been pregnant and it was just a baby. He said, "Ronnie, it was not a baby. It was your younger sister, Vikki. She was murdered. They finally found her after two weeks of being missing."

This moment shattered my life, as well as my dreams for the future. To make a long story short, for my family has never found closure to this death, for the murder was never solved. It was the first time that I had ever been confronted with death. The hardest question that I have ever had to answer was the question that my mother addressed to me and my brother Karl. Being the oldest boys, she asked us if we wanted our sister to have a casket, and if so what kind. This question forced us both to realize that our sister had been murdered.

At the funeral, which we had decided was to be closed casket; I said my good-byes to my sister. That is when I gave up on God! I could not understand how God could let something like this happen to a seventeen-year-old girl. In my heart I knew there was no God, and if there was, I didn't want anything to do with Him. This was the second time that God had come into my life and thoughts, and I hated Him!

My third significant experience with God's presence came five years after my sister died. A lot had transpired in my life since then. I had finished my last two years in the navy, I resigned my supervisor position. I did not go to officer school, so I did not fly F-14s. I gave up all hope of being a U.S. senator. My dreams and goals were all gone. I had seen the life taken out of my mother and watched her cry many days, especially around my sister's birthday. The life was taken completely out of my family. I myself hated everything and everybody. There was no love in me or around me.

I had entered life on the streets and a life of hustling, and I enjoyed every bit of it. I had had a nervous breakdown, but nobody knew it. Why? Because I did not care about myself or others, and I felt in my heart there was no God. I needed to try to find a way out of the nightmare I had been living for five years. Awake or asleep, my sister's death was there in my mind daily.

My mom had found Christ in her life and had given me a Bible. I took the Bible for sentimental reasons and because she was my mom. I put it in my car and never read it; it did nothing for me as it just gathered dust. She had found Christ, not me; I didn't want anything to do with him.

Late one particular evening, my friends and I was throwing around a football. My friend Spanky threw me the ball. He threw so well he could have been an NFL quarterback if given the chance, but he hadn't, so instead he resorted to hustling, like me. Spanky and I were discussing taking off work—hustling was our job—and going to the Cool Jazz Festival the following week in Houston. We decided to go and discussed the plan before parting ways for the night.

The next morning, I was informed that Spanky had been robbed and murdered, his body thrown into the bushes. I thought to myself, here we go again. Would I end up like this? Is this the way people die? Shortly thereafter, I drove to Fort Worth and attended Spanky's funeral. There, God's voice began to talk with me, telling me that if I did not change my life, my family would be attending my funeral. I had heard the voice when no one else heard it.

I left Texas, for all this was too much for me. I went to San Diego, California. I was beginning to see things differently, but I still hated God. For a while I lived at a hotel in Point Loma California. The Billy Graham crusades program was on for two nights. I did not want to watch it, but I did, not knowing why. He was preaching from the book of Revelations, and I was listening. He not only scared me from his preaching and talking about the four horsemen, but he was able to make me think about my coming days. I just knew that the world was coming to an end that first night.

I woke up the next day, and the world was still there. I could not wait to see Billy again. That night was his second night of teaching on the book of Revelation. I listened intensely, and I knew that God was speaking to me. He was speaking to my heart. At the conclusion of His message, I opened the Bible that my mother had given me to the twenty-third psalm. I did not understand a word of it; it said something like, "The Lord is my shepherd, and I should not want." The words were very difficult for me. I could not relate to the words; I felt I was not a sheep, I was a human. What did I need a shepherd for? I read all the way down to the sixth verse. The chapter spoke of goodness and mercy. I had no idea what these two words meant; I knew what money and drugs and good times were, but never had I experienced goodness and mercy in my life. Even though these words were foreign to me, my eye struck something I did know. The word *all,* and that *all* meant I would have this goodness and the mercy for eternity—all the rest of the days of my life. This was good enough for me, and so I gave my heart to God and surrendered my life to Christ. My life has never been the same ever since that night

The fourth time God entered my life directly was when He spoke to me on September 30, 2000. I can remember the experience as if it was yesterday. I wrote this book because of this experience, and I wrote it for you, whoever and wherever you are. I had suffered a near-fatal aneurism in the brain stem in my neck and a stroke on my right side. I was not expected to live. It placed me in a coma.

While I was unconscious, my mind was in a unique place. There was only a room with no form or shape and featuring a door that would not open for me. I was there for three days. While I was in the coma, God spoke to me and said, "We have decided that you must go back. Your work is not finished." At that moment, the door opened. I came out of the coma, opened my eyes, and have been "awakened" ever since.

This book is about that journey of mine from ignorance to awakening. It is for everyone, whether they have given their life to Christ and have decided to follow Him, or whether they are still searching for the answers they seek in this life. It is especially for the physically challenged souls of this world; I hope that this book will inspire such persons to never give up hope. A disability is not the end for you; it is only the beginning of a new part of your journey.

This book strives to assure you that there is something in the invisible that is there for you and that all the answers you have been looking for will be found. It is meant to remind you to always live the life that you are supposed to live. May this book awaken your spirit and your soul such that you may find and discover the life, the way, and the truth of your being.

My final note for you: do not read this book like all the other books you have read. It is not to be *read*; it is to be absorbed into your life. Review a chapter at a time and reflect on what you have read, for it is a true story. Reflect on your own life before moving to the next chapter. My hope is that you are awakened from this day on and that you enjoy the rest of your journey through life until you reach your final destination in Heaven. I will see you there, for it does exist, and that is where our true journey begins.

Ronnie V. Broadus

Chapter One

Life Before the Awakening

I would like say before beginning this story that I hope and pray that you may experience the wonderful awakening that I have encountered in this life. My journey began many years ago. I would even say that my journey began when I was in my mother's womb, at the conception of my life. Even through my many encounters along this course we call life, this particular part of my journey stands out above the rest.

Before the turmoil I went through that is described in the introduction, I became a very successful businessman—according to man's measurement of success in business. Over the ensuing years, I had set goals in my life and had reached them. This description of my past is rather egotistical, for that is the way I was, how I had become. I was in sales all my adult life, some twenty years, mostly in the cemetery and insurance businesses. I had developed retail locations (carts) in several different shopping malls in San Diego, California.

I also was a leading member at my church, the Mount Zion Missionary Baptist Church, and was constantly striving for excellence in my life. Every three months or so, I would leave the United States and go to some foreign country or other in an effort to spread the Gospel and the Great Commission of our Lord and savior Jesus Christ. Why did I do this? I guess I am a little different than most people; you see, I love the Lord passionately. I had figured out a long time before I started making such pilgrimages that I wanted God in my life and that I wanted to carry out the Great Commission, which we are required to do. As you can see from my success in business, I was quite a busy person, but I was very unhappy because I had learned that not all money was good money.

What I mean to say is that you can make a lot of money in business, have a nice home, a nice car, and all sorts of things, but that does not guarantee you happiness or success in life. At one point in my life, I had neither success nor happiness, even though I was doing all of the things that I thought it was right to do with my life. In reality, I was only doing busy work and running around in circles. I was only living ordinary life and not the abundant life that Christ had promised me. Anyway, I had prayed to God asking how I could be a Christian and follow Jesus yet remain in business, for it is commonly thought that all business people are evil and immoral. Theoretically, any good Christian, therefore, cannot and should not be in business, because its primarily source of money is people. How can you be in sales without contact with people? So this was quite a dilemma for me; I wanted to serve God and carry out the Great Commission, for I had been called to be an evangelist, and it was my duty and charge to carry my purpose for living to completion. Yet at the same time, I was in a career that was considered by many to be quite sinful. So as I said, I prayed, petitioning God to place me in a ministry that I might build a Christian business and carry out the Great Commission at the same time.

My prayers were answered. I was told to build a network of businesses that would provide the resources to operate the ministry. I was very puzzled by this answer, because I knew how hard it was to get people to give their money to God, and this is one area in which I fall short of the glory of God—I hate with a passion to ask anyone for money to finance God's program or for His kingdom building on the planet earth. For how can you not give to God when has done so much for you?

My life was so busy, for I was working day and night in the business, both for the business itself and to make the necessary resources to establish the ministry so I might save souls for the Lord—and let us not forget to also provide the daily necessities of life. I succeeded in earning enough revenues from the business to not only support me but also the ministry. I always maintained my belief that God would provide for me and guide me and the ministry through the journey and that he would never go back on his word.

I was called into the ministry and preached my first sermon in February of 1983. Even though I preached many sermons, I had no clear direction for my life or any idea what my exact purpose was in the household of faith. I was called reverend by the congregation, but I was not a pastor. I simply waited patiently on God, for I really did not want to be a pastor; I felt in my heart that I was not called to such an office. Even though all my ministry friends were pastors, I knew that I was just a preacher, and that was just fine with me. I preferred to just preach the Word of God and not have all the additional problems and burdens that came with being a pastor.

Some time latter in my journey, the Holy Spirit spoke to me. I was sitting in church, so it was Sunday morning. My pastor was preaching, and I was listening to the morning message. As I was listening, I heard a voice say to me, "Ronnie, I am well pleased with you, and I am going to give you the desires of your heart." The voice told me that I had been called to be an evangelist and that I would go all over the world, preaching the Gospel.

Because I knew that we are all constantly listening for a voice to listen to and because I had never heard of a black preacher going all over the world preaching the Gospel, I figured that God had the wrong guy. I was nowhere close to Billy Graham, so I said aloud, "Satan, get behind me." The voice stopped.

I was riding in my car that week with confusion in my heart, and I asked God if that was truly Him talking with me at church the past Sunday. If it was, I asked Him to give me another chance, if this was to be so.

The rest of the week went by, and I was back at church listening to the pastor once more bringing his Sunday morning message. The voice came again and said, "Ronnie, I am well pleased with you, and I will give you the desires of your heart. You have been called to be an evangelist, and you will preach my Gospel all over the world."

This time I only said, "Yes, Lord."

My life has never been the same since. Everything that the Holy Spirit told me that day has come to pass. I have been to Russia on two occasions, Africa on four occasions, India on two occasions, and Peru on two occasions. That's a total of nine years of evangelism that I have spent in foreign countries. God has allowed me to minister and preach his Gospel, in turn saving souls throughout the world. What is truly wonderful about accepting His service is that though it is not over yet, when it is over, He will return, as His Word proclaims.

I've had to tell you all of this in order to bring you where I was in my journey when I had my true awakening. My life as a successful Christian businessman was fabulous. I worked long hours, and I acquired the resources that fueled my ministry so I could carry out God's plan for my life. My days began and ended in representing clients in cemetery negotiations or in the insurance industry as I operated four retail locations in the malls of San Diego and managed the employees for all these operations. Such was my life before the awakening.

Chapter Two

The Awakening

Humpty Dumpty sat on the wall, and Humpty Dumpty had a great fall. All the king's horses and all the king's men could not put Humpty Dumpty back together again.

You are probably wondering why Humpty Dumpty was on the wall. Also, why did he fall? And why couldn't the king's men put him back together? My belief is that Humpty was just where he was supposed to be in his journey in life. He was on the wall, not knowing that he was soon to fall off the wall, and yet sure enough he fell, just as many of us fall off the road of the human experience.

All the king's horses and all the king's men couldn't put Humpty Dumpty back together again because he was shattered! When we are shattered, cracked in a thousand pieces, the parts do not easily fit back together. I have learned that there are some things we run into in the human experience, in this journey that we call life, that no one can help us with. It does not matter who you have depended on in the past, or what you have done for others in the past, or how you have lived your life in the past, or whether you are good or bad. There are some things, events, occurrences—whatever you want to call them—that are stoppers of your journey that can bring your life to a standstill or a crash. This is what occurred to Humpty Dumpty when he was shattered. How do I know this? Because once, I was Humpty Dumpty.

Many people feel that all days are the same. I use to feel that way, organizing my days, my weeks, and my years. I figured that I had seventy years to live, according to the scriptures. I would often start my days not thinking about tomorrow, as if I had all the time in the world. I would go on about my business, knowing that I was a son of God, walking in faith, and knowing that I was in the Father's hand.

I started September 30, 2000, just as I had started any other day. I was forty-five years of age and was expecting a birthday in two months. As usual, I had planned my day the night before, and I would carry out my plan and goals for that day to perfection. I was unaware that this was the last day of my life on the planet earth. It was a Friday, and it started like any other day. My routine was to pick up supplies for the carts and deliver the supplies to all the carts in the various malls of San Diego, staying at each for a couple of hours before moving to the next. After the carts were serviced, I would then move on to service my clients in the cemetery and insurance industries. These activities would usually take me about eight hours to complete, and most of my days were little different from the pattern. Occasionally I would go and stand an eight-hour shift at one of the malls in order to cut the labor costs of running the business.

I was positioned at the alpine location that fateful Friday evening making phone calls to the other locations to see how they had done for the day, as was typical. I closed the Alpine location at about 9:30 p.m. and took my nightly drive to San Diego to close the final two locations in the city. I had a slight headache, but I figured it was probably stress related. I was making my normal calls on my cell phone as I was driving, as if I had all the time in the world.

I would often go to the movies at night, for working on weekends and all through the day did not allow me to see movies during daylight hours. There was a movie that I had been waiting to see, *Remember the Titans* with Denzel Washington. I later would come to believe that I was predestined to see this movie.

So after closing up my retail locations, I decided that I would go to that movie. The movie lasted a couple of hours. I always enjoyed late movies; they gave me time to wind down from a long day of work. When the movie was over, I started driving from Chula Vista. On the way, I made a phone call to my assistant, Erika, requesting that I might pick up the payments from that night's receipts, for she had worked at one of the locations in San Diego that night. As I reached her home in Bonita, we discussed that day's activities, the events that had occurred within the business that day, the problems that had occurred throughout the day, and the possible problems that might occur over the next week or so. We decided to cut our meeting short, though, when I began to complain about my growing headache. I did not know that this was nearly the end of my last day on the earth.

As I was leaving Erika's home, my head was throbbing with pain. It hurt so bad that I remember asking her if I could sit on her steps for a little while. I felt dizzy. Her apartment was on the second floor. As I sat there, my head was really hurting, but I felt that if I could just get home and lie down I would be fine. I had had plenty of headaches before, but I must say none this bad. As I sat on the steps, I began to feel slightly better—enough to try to get to my truck. I managed to lift myself up off the ground with the help of the rail. As I was going down the stairs, I held tightly onto the rail so to keep my balance and so I would not fall. As I got to the bottom of the stairs, however, I stopped because I knew that something was wrong.

I felt that if I was to move one more step, I would fall to the ground. At this point I called to Erika, who was standing at the top of the stairs, to come and help me get to my truck. This was another signal that something was seriously wrong and hindering me, because I am the type of man that didn't ever need any help. I always said I would do it myself—that way I knew that it would get done. The walk down Erika's breezeway was one of the longest walks I had ever taken in my life, but with her help, we finally made it to my truck.

As I was opening the door and trying to get into the truck, I quickly realized that I could not feel anything on my right side. I could not even step up into the truck. Still, I said nothing, not wanting to alarm my assistant. At this point, though, I began to do something very unusual for me, and something that I hate with a passion. I began vomiting and could not stop.

At this point I told Erika to call my youngest brother, Karron, right away. If I was vomiting—something I almost never do—I knew in my heart that something was terribly wrong. I requested that she laid me on the ground, and I would rest while she made the call. She was unable to contact him, which upset me. I really needed to reach him. I don't know even to this day where he was or what he was doing. After failing to contact him, I decided that we had best try to contact an ambulance, which meant calling 911. By this point I knew not only that something was wrong, but that I was running out of time. How I knew this, I don't know, but I knew I had to act, and I needed to act now!

Erika called 911 immediately. As I lay there on the ground, I believe my assistant's neighbors came driving up, for I remember a man consoling me and telling me to lay still. I was still vomiting repeatedly. Everything that was in me, I mean everything, was now coming out of my system. It felt like I had thrown up my heart, kidneys, intestines, stomach—everything that is inside a human being.

Shortly I could hear the ambulance's siren looking for me, still on the ground in the parking lot behind my truck, for I never made it inside my truck. The ambulance finally found me, how I don't know. I heard the paramedics asking questions. The one question I remember is the one where they asked if I was drunk. Can you believe that? They actually thought I had been drinking! I remember being incredulous about that at the time, but I guess because I was vomiting still, that their reasoning could have made sense. None of us knew at that point that I was having an aneurysm that would lead to a brain stem stroke.

I think this is a good time to take a pause along this journey to recap and to give my interpretation of what has happened. I have come to learn and believe that we should stop along our journeys to see where we are and to reflect. It is unfortunate that I have had to learn this wisdom the hard way, through the human experiences I have had to go through—many that I hope that you will not have to undergo to learn this type of wisdom.

I mentioned earlier that there are some things, events, or life occurrences that can cause you to crash or even be shattered. I was entering a crash zone on my journey and did not know it. I did not recognize that I was about to be shattered; I assumed that everything was going just, as I had plan, and that I was on the road to success and a prosperous life. I have come to believe that we are not in control of the journey we are on, nor can we control the place where we should be. We only have some control over the place where we are going.

And that is only a half of the whole. Life is not completely about the destination, but it is also about the journey—a journey that has many roads and turns in its highways and byways, which can change at any moment. My thoughts and ideas are mine and have not come from someone else's thoughts. They are mine, and they are based on my journey. I thought everything was fine in my life and felt that I was in control of my own journey. I soon realized that I was not in control; the human experience was actually in control. For this journey, this life, this experience, is a new experience that has never been written or told.

We enter this world, this journey, and we depart this journey when it is time to depart. There is nothing that we can do to alter this course. My advice, which I have come to understand through the long hours of thought, is to love God with all your heart, mind, and soul. Love your neighbor as yourself, and love your family and children while you can, for our lives are as a vapor and can be over in a moment's time. As I mentioned earlier, it does not matter how good you have been in your eyesight or what you have done for others. What does matter is how you have lived your life up to this point in your journey, for it does not end—it is eternal.

To continue the story of my journey, as I said, the ambulance had arrived. I still lay there on the ground. As the paramedics placed me on their stretcher, I was still vomiting. They placed me in the ambulance. I remember telling my assistant to take my truck and follow us to the hospital, for inside of me was great fear. I did not know what was going on, but I knew something had happened.

As I was placed in the ambulance, the attendant was working on me. I don't remember if it was a man or woman paramedic, but I do remember being in the ambulance and seeing the paramedics. One went to the front and one was in the back of the ambulance with me. I believe the paramedic gave me a shot of something to stop me from vomiting, but I didn't. However, soon I did lose consciousness. I did not know what was happening to me, but I knew *something* was happening to me and that I was now in God's hand, for I had no control of the journey.

I regained consciousness but did not know where I was. I remembered being placed in an ambulance, but the environment around me now did not look like an ambulance. It did not look like an emergency room, either, so I believed I had gone threw the whole process of being admitted to the hospital, gone through the emergency, and later I had been moved to an ICU room, all while I was unconscious.

As I woke up, I began to vomit again. I looked around the room, the ICU room, and I saw my younger brother, Karron, and my assistant, Erika. I was thrilled that she had located my brother, who is very dear to me. I motioned to him to come near me. I remember telling him that I was sorry that we had not gotten to accomplish the goals that we were trying to complete for him, for he was an aspiring NBA player. He had spent half his life playing basketball and going to basketball camps after he had finished college.

So I told him what I had to say to him, and to this day I don't know why I said what I said to him. I felt that I was going to die; as a matter of fact, I knew in my heart that I was dying and that this would probably be the last time ever that I would be talking with him, for I was going to see the Lord.

I must tell you now that I believe in Angels. I first read about them in my Bible, and since they were in the Bible, you didn't have to tell me a second time that they existed. It is in the Word of God—just as there is a

Heaven and a Hell, or Life and Death, I believe it to be because the Word of God says so. Even though I have never seen or experienced Heaven or Hell, I know they are there, as I have accepted that by faith.

The reason I mention Angels is because two of them visited me to comfort me. After I saw my brother, I fell back into an unconscious state. I was cold, very cold. I was also afraid. Usually I was not afraid of anything, but on this occasion, I was. As I opened my eyes again, I saw that I was in a room by myself—at least I thought I was. The environment was strange, and I knew that I was in a hospital room. I was lying on a bed scared out of my mind. I guess I was scared in part because I did not know exactly where I was.

While I was focusing my eyesight, I felt a presence in the room with me. There was a woman in the room with me. She asked me if I was all right. I told her that I was cold; she said she would make me warm, and she did, but I never saw a blanket or a sheet. Nevertheless, I was now very warm and comfortable, but I was scared. The lady asked me what was wrong. I told her I was scared and asked her to pray for me, and she said she would. After this request, I never saw her again.

On another occasion, I opened my eyes to see I was in the hospital room all by myself and began to cry, because I did not know what was happening and I was not in control. I began to yell for someone, but it seemed that no one was there. Then I heard a voice, and I knew this voice. It was my cousin's voice. I asked him how long he had been there and when he had arrived. He said that he had been with me all the time since I had arrived at the hospital and that I should get some rest. I said I felt comfortable knowing that he was there with me. What I forgot to ask him was how he got from the state of Georgia to California.

I believe that these were two Angels that were assigned to me, to be with me and protect me even in death. The Bible says that Angels come to you unaware. Well all I know is that there were two people with me on those occasions that I have never seen again. I made later inquiries about the whereabouts of the lady visitor and was told that there was no such person on duty or at the hospital. I also later talked with my cousin, who told me he was praying for me but was unable to come to California. I've thought about these moments of my life many times, and the only conclusion I can come up with is that these really were Angels sent to protect me. What made this difficult to believe for me is that I did not know there were both male and female Angels. I had never believed that there were woman Angels, but we must believe God at this level and accept His revelations in our lives. If there are men and women on this plane, why can't there be both man and woman Angels? I can say more about this subject, but this is not the time or place for it. Regardless, I do know now that a woman Angel came and comforted me when I truly needed someone with me.

This is the part of my journey that I hope makes all who think that death is the end of one's life reconsider. I would like to tell you about my death. None have ever seen death or been to Heaven or Hell and can report about experiencing this event that we all must go through, for we are yet walking, talking, breathing humans that have not entered the eternal bliss that God has in store for us. But I pray that what you are about to read will affect your life as deeply as the events have affected mine. I have learned, and now believe, that death is not the end of your life, but only your, beginning of something very new, so new that you have never experience it before, but you will experience, something new and marvelous..

I awoke and could see all around me. I did not know where I was, nor did I recognize my surroundings. I was in a room all by myself. The room was all white but was shapeless—no corners or windows—but there was a door with a doorknob. The room had no floor, no walls, no ceiling.

Even though I was viewing this strange place, I was not afraid at all. I was at perfect peace with myself. I had quit vomiting, and I felt no pain. I was fully dressed and sitting on a floor that wasn't there, just looking at the door. I wondered where I was and why there were no windows in this place, only a door, and why this room was so white, and why the door was there, and where this door led. My thoughts were many and clear.

My brothers and sisters, I have thought about what happened to me in this room for the last six years of my life. It is something that God has placed in my heart to remember and share with you—a reminder that He is in charge of life and death and that you should never fear death, for He has overcome it. As I was sitting there looking at the door, my curiosity began to take over. That is just how I was created; I am one of those people that wants to know why. My major in college was behavioral science, and people like me are prone to asking questions—who, what, why, and where.

So I sat there wondering what this door was and why it was there. Was this the door the one I had read about in my Bible, the door of knowledge? Or was this the door that if I knocked, if I sought, I would find? Many thoughts were racing through my mind. I stood up from my seated position and decided that I would go over to the door and try to open it to see what was behind it. As I started to walk to the door, I realized I was not actually walking, but I was floating. Nevertheless, I reached the door, and as I touched the doorknob, I felt a shock. I immediately let the doorknob go, for I still had feeling in my body, and I was hurled backward, literally turning backward flips until I was back to where I had been sitting.

Why was I floating and flipping? I soon realized that the room was like space. I was weightless, like an astronaut. I could not get out this formless room, which frightened me, for I did not know where I was or what was happening to me. So I did nothing for a time.

Later, after I had built up enough courage, I floated to the door and tried to open it once again. Unfortunately, I got the same result. I repeated this process of going to the door, getting shocked, and being hurled back to my original spot at least four times. I simply could not open the door. I don't know what made me get up and try the door over and over again—maybe persistence, I don't know—but I went to the door one more time. As I approached this time, something different happened. My hand stayed on the doorknob, I did not get shocked, nor was I hurled backward.

At that moment, I heard a voice in the room with me. It said, "We have decided that you will go back. Your work has not been completed." The door opened, and as I went through it, I heard the voice say to me, "Preach the Gospels to all the nations and baptize them in the Holy Ghost."

At that very moment of time, I came out of the coma. I was in a hospital bed. There was a woman in front of me whom I thought was my wife, Brendolyn, but it was my daughter, Christy, who looks exactly like her mother. I discovered later that she had refused to go home from the hospital, because she knew her father was in a coma and wanted to be there if I woke up. She was not going to believe the doctors' report that I had only a 20 percent chance of living.

I said, "Hi, baby."

She thought she had seen a ghost. She ran out the room to get the nurse and tell her that I had woken up and then got on the phone to tell my relatives that I had awakened from the coma. I did not know until then that I had been in a coma for three straight days.

Chapter Three

The ICU Room

Later in the ICU room I talked with my younger brother, Karron, he was in the ICU room, with me. I knew in my heart that this was the last time that I would ever talk with him. I was leaving this world, and I knew it. The fact that I was dying was not an issue with me, for I knew that I had lived a righteous life. I knew that I had not lived a perfect life, but I had lived a good and full one, not only by faith, but in service of God and not myself.

The thought in my mind, like in many people's minds, was that I was sick and that something was horribly wrong. Even though I felt this way. I knew that the doctor, would prescribe some medications, tell my family to make sure I get plenty of rest, and release me from the Hospital. I also felt that the doctors and nurses would fix me up and I would be home the next day, I felt this way because, I never got sick and I believed that I was blessed, favored by God and anointed by God to preach the Gospel. I felt that I was living the abundant life. I also knew that no sickness could lord over my body, so whatever was happening or whatever I was coming up against could not have any power over me. But now, my journey was saying something else. I thought I was done for.

After waking up and then seeing Christy run out the room, I lay in the bed wondering where I was. My mind had many thoughts upon it, because it was now going back into the mode of running my body. I wondered where I had been; it was like going to sleep and waking up from that sleep without knowing where you were, only awakening to a new day. I was told later that I had been unconscious for three days, though to me it seemed like no more than a couple of hours. Anyway, my mind was trying to figure out what had happened. Listen—I thought I had been placed in purgatory. Now, I had heard of purgatory or read about it, but I didn't know if it really existed.

I have always believed that if you had a relationship with the Lord, He would take care of you and He would talk to you and give you all the answers that you needed. You just had to be still and know that He is God and in control of your life. Well, I had been completely still, and in the hospital I still was. So I decided right there in that bed to ask God, for I knew that it did not matter where you were to talk with God, because God is everywhere—and I mean *everywhere*. So I asked, "God, where have I been? What has been going on, and what is going on?"

He did not give me an answer then, but He did answer. He always answers us when we are ready to accept the answer, for He is not a respecter of His children, meaning He treats us all the same. There are no little *you*s and big *me*s in God's house.

When He did answer, I heard the voice as clear as day. It said that I had been placed in the room for my own safety until a decision had been made about me. I wasn't able to leave that place until the decision had been made, and also, my body needed the time to repair itself. The Lord shared with me that the decision was too involved for me to understand, but it had to do with me going to Heaven or going back to earth in order that I might finish my work there.

This reply really startled me, for I was happy where I was on earth. I was totally at peace with myself, and my mind was very clear. It turned out that the decision had been made to send me back to complete the work that I had been called to do in my lifetime and with my generation. I was told this as I lay in the hospital bed. This reiterated what I already knew: that no one can die or would die until God said so; we do not have a choice. After that, I fell asleep again.

When I woke from my sleep, I found myself lying in the hospital bed again. This area was called the intensive care unit (ICU), though those words really didn't mean anything to me at this time. I did not know that I had been there since that Friday night and it was now Sunday—what part of Sunday I did not know—but this was the day that God had allowed me to awaken from my sleep. Now, conscious, everything seemed the same and looked the same. At this time, I felt really rested, so I knew that whatever had happened, I must really have needed the sleep. All I knew was that it was now time for me to get out the bed, get discharged from this hospital, get home, and get to my business, for it needed me. Then I noticed that I was seeing two of everything and that I was tied to the bed. I had been so sedated that I didn't pay much attention to these things until now, when I tried to get up for the first time.

As I lay there in the hospital bed, people began to come into the room. It sort of took on the form of a dream, for I had not seen some of these people for quite some time. Only a short while had passed since I had seen Christy, and now I was seeing other loved ones, family members, and close friends who had heard I was in the hospital and unconscious.

The first person that I saw and recognized was my oldest brother, Karl. At this moment I really did think I was dreaming. I had just visited Karl a week earlier, in Washington State, and I wondered what he was doing in this room. The second face that I recognized was my mother, Mrs. Earline D. Taylor. I wondered what she was doing here. She lived in, Temple, Texas. She later told me that upon hearing of my condition, Southwest Airlines had delayed a plane's departure so she could get on that plane to come. (Isn't God good?) I felt again that I must be dreaming, for it had been many years since I had seen my mother and Karl in the same place.

Then I saw my wife, Brendolyn Broadus. She was smiling and crying at the same time, and I did not know why. At this time I asked for my younger brother, Karron, thinking that I was actually talking. But my speech had left, and I was only mumbling. My family hadn't told me that I could not talk, but understood what I was trying to say anyway. Sure enough, my younger brother was there, and it was good to see him. I have always tried to look after Karron; that's the way our mother has raised us, to always look after one another. She would always say, "All we have is one another." It was just like me—I guess it is in my nature—to be coming out of a coma and instead of worrying about myself, I was worrying about others.

I then asked for Erika, my sister in Christ and my friend. She also served as my assistant to my business and the ministry. I tried to speak again, but nothing came out. I realized my muteness this time and was alarmed but said nothing. I figured I was just tired. My brother Karl made a list of the alphabet on a sheet of paper to assist me. He would ask me a question, and I would answer by pointing at the letters in turn. By spelling the answer, I was able to more easily communicate with him and the others. I remember him saying that I was going to be all right, because I could still spell, meaning that my mind was still working and that I had not lost the use of it. Karl had some knowledge in this area because worked with stroke victims at the Veterans Administration in Washington. He was not only a blessing to me, but being the first born of my mother's children, he was also a blessing to the family. I did not know at the time, that sickness affects the entire family structure. What I mean by this, is that when a sickness or even death, occurs in, a family, it affects the entire family circle, it changes everything, when I say everything, it not only affects the one whom is sick or have died, but it will changes the family structure, forever, and it happens over night. The family knows, in their heart, that a loss has occurred, and their life, will never be the same. I have learned this through my experience with sickness.

By then I was awake enough again to have an awareness of who and where I was, even though I was tied to the bed. I knew that something was wrong, because my mother and brother were there. I immediately passed the operations of the business and the ministry over to Erika. Most people did not understand this move, but I did. I knew that the business and the ministry were our bread and butter, and they had to be protected at all costs. I knew by now that I was down and did not know for how long, for I had not met with any doctors yet.

I caught some static from my family over the appointment, but they did not work in my business and did not know how to run it. They felt I should have had Brendolyn, my wife, run all the operations, but I knew that Brendolyn was highly emotional about me, and she was also a heart patient and was in line for kidney dialysis. The business would be too much for her, and I knew it.

I thank God for Erika, for she was my assistant, and she not only took on the business and ministry, but God saw fit for her to save my life by calling 911 that Friday night. I will always be eternally grateful to her. Thank God for training; I do believe in it.

As everyone was crying and smiling around me, I watched them and made various gestures to them, communicating as best I could. Shortly, the nurse came into the crowded room. She told everyone to leave the room, because I needed the rest. They were allowed to come by and see me later.

Soon I fell asleep again, and I was awakened by movement. My bed was moving as I was being removed from the ICU ward to the rehabilitation ward. I remember the bed coming to a stop in a hallway. My primary doctor, Dr. Jerome Robinson—whom I am eternally grateful to, also—was talking to me. I could only listen as he said to me, "Well, you're in bad shape, but with time, we will put you back together."

As he admitted me to the rehabilitation unit, I said, "Okay Doctor Robinson," without knowing what kind of shape I was in. After mumbling these words, I fell back to sleep. I did not know my future. "I did not know what my future held, but I knew that my life had been changes."

Chapter Four

The Hospital

What were my thoughts at this time in my journey? Honestly, things were going so fast, it was like watching a movie. One moment I was running a prosperous business, the next moment I was vomiting continuously, then riding in the ambulance, being admitted to the hospital, falling into a coma, and the next thing I knew I was waking up out of a coma and seeing people I had not seen in quite some time. This was all unbearable to take, but I must truly say that I was not scared through most of the experience. I had reached a place in God's presence, a place of comfort. I had reached a place of serenity that only God can give. I will also tell you that all through this process, I never felt any pain beyond that initial headache. Isn't God good?

Let's continue the journey. Upon, awakening from my sleep. I soon realize that this day, would, be a day, like no other days that I had experience I was in a different room and I was in a room by myself, but I was still in a hospital bed, and I soon realize, that this was not the ICU room. I had been moved to another room but I am still tied to the bed—what for, I don't know. It's a big room with four beds in it and a private bathroom with a shower, which I would see later. But the room had no windows. I soon realized that I was still at the hospital. As I lay there in the bed wondering what was going on, a lady came into the room. She addressed me using my last name, which gave me reason to be alarmed, for all my friends called me by my first name, Ronnie. I asked her who she was, though it was difficult because I was slurring every word or trying to remember proper words of speech. She said that I had been admitted in the Paradise Valley Stroke Rehabilitation Unit and that she was my nurse. I was silent, and she went on to say that my doctors would be by soon to tell me what had transpired. I was stunned, concerned, amazed, as well as disturbed; after all, I was not in control. Whatever had happened to me was now in control of my life. I could only depend on what I believed in, for I was truly being tested, and I felt it would take everything that I believed in to get through this test.

As I lay there, a doctor I had never met before came in and started asking me questions and putting me through movements to see how I would respond. At this time I still did not know what exactly had happened to me. The doctor then began to fill me in. He said that on September 30, 2000, I had suffered a central pontine hemorrhagic stroke. He also told me that the stroke had put me in a coma for three days, and immediately upon gaining consciousness, I had been unable to speak, walk, or eat. He said I was paralyzed on my right side, pointing out that my right hand was curled up. My gait, speech, vision, and equilibrium were all impaired.

This was a lot for me to grasp. I received it in silence and thought of the others it would affect. I did realize the gravity of the situation, but I knew that this news would affect others' lives, not just mine, for many people depended on my business and my ministry, as well. Even though the news was disappointing, I knew that the scriptures said that because of Jesus's suffering, I was healed. At that moment, that was all that mattered to me. What the doctor had told me did not matter; Jesus had died for me on Calvary's cross, and so no matter what was going on with my health, I was healed from the effects of that. I felt that I was going to get up in a couple of days and walk right out of that hospital.

I later found out that there were two other doctors that God had placed in my life during a time that I really needed them. I would not be telling you of my journey if not for Drs. Oscar Guzman and William Chapman, and I will be eternally grateful for them both.

When I had regained consciousness and was told that I could not talk or walk, I was truly scared, even though I could not show it. Anyway, the fear would not help anyone, including myself. But I must tell you, there is a great fear that comes over you when you receive devastating news, and at that point in your life you must make the decision of whether you are going to go on, or you are going to stay where you are and feel sorry for yourself. My decision was not to feel sorry for myself. Even though I was in bad shape and could not do anything about my current situation, I was going to trust God. For after all, He was the one that created me, and if He created me, He could fix me.

I was facing giants and their little brothers in my life, but I knew there was a God, and He was at the head of my life. Even though I was facing giants, I knew that Joshua and Caleb had faced giants in their own lives and were victorious because of how they saw the situation. My perception of my situation was quite bleak. I was in the wilderness, but I felt and knew that God was walking with me through the wilderness and that somehow I would get through this season of my life. I knew that I had done too much good with my life. I had paid the tithe, given the offering, taught Sunday school, and gone on many mission trips for the Lord. I felt that my life could not end here and in this situation, for there was still work for me to do. I kept in my mind that the Word of God said that because Christ hung on the cross for me, I was healed from all sickness. I was in a place in my life where I believed it, and had to believe it. I felt that I must hold on to my faith and not believe the fleeting, temporal things that I was seeing and feeling.

The bad news was not over; it seems that when it rains, it truly does pour. As I lay in my hospital room contemplating my issues and wondering how this was going to turn out, I was also informed that I would probably be unable to secure gainful occupation due to my disability. What an awful word, *disability*. I had entered the world of the disabled person, whom I have a multitude of respect for, having become disabled myself. It is not a pretty world, but I say hang in their disabled persons! You will make it!

Since the brain stem stroke was on the left side of my brain at the base of my neck, it had affected the right side of my body and motor functions. I had complete paralysis on my right side. The damage, I was told, would seriously affect my ability to walk. Worse, I was also told that I would have severe limitations to my right upper extremity, with weakness and frequent tremors. This is pretty depressing stuff, isn't it? But I am not finished. I was told that I also had a brain disorder, resulting in depressed moods, anxiety, suspiciousness, panic attacks, chronic sleep impairment, impaired judgment, impairment of short- and long-term memory, impaired abstract thinking, disturbance of motivation, difficulty in establishing and maintaining effective work and social relationships, and other cognitive difficulties. That's what I mean when I say that I had giants *and* their little brothers in my life! They were surrounding me and trying to capture my soul, but I knew in my heart that God was with me and that in some kind of way, God was going to work things out in my favor. God was still at the head of my life, no matter what I was hearing or seeing or feeling. God was still in control, for I was still breathing, and I was still alive.

Let me tell you about my faith. I always knew that faith was the substance of things hoped for and the evidence of things not seen. But at this time in my life, I was in a place in my consciousness where I only had faith in God's Word. I knew was blessed and highly favored and that I had to hold on to my faith. My faith was at the point where I knew that God was going to step in and heal my body, and I was going to go home. I was going to be one of God's miracles, for I believed the Word and that He would do this for me. I was one of His children, and I believed that God did not want me to worry about anything, but the reality of my situation said something altogether different. Still, I knew that I could only rest in His love for me, trust in His direction for me, and believe that no matter how things looked, it was going to be all right.

Continuing on in my journey, I was informed by my nurse that a meeting was being set up for me. Based on the decisions of the doctors, I would either be released from the hospital to go home, or I would stay at the hospital for more care and rehabilitation. The meeting included my speech therapist, my physical therapist, my occupational therapist, my mother, my doctors, and my wife, who was shattered by this whole experience and could not believe what had happened or make any decisions. I believe she was in shock, for I was not only her husband of twenty years, but I was also her best friend. Because of this, my mother had to make all the decisions. Nor did I have the ability to make these decisions—ones that I was at the heart of. I had no say in the matter, for I was a patient of the hospital and my rights had been given up.

Leading up to the meeting, I was very nervous because I just wanted to go home and heal up and go run my businesses. I needed to go about my life and it would be fine, for I was a Christian, an evangelist, a businessman, an employer, a husband, a provider, and I was on my church's staff., and I believed the Word. How could they keep me there? I was too important not only to a large amount of people, but also to kingdom building and to God. I had not accepted the fact that I had been in a coma for three days, had suffered a major stroke in my brain stem, was paralyzed on my right side, and had double vision. Yes, I saw two of everybody; now that was different.

I remember having a conversation—with the help of pen and paper—with my mom and telling her what I wanted her to say at the meeting. It was only appropriate for me to have a voice, but I would have to speak through her. With my disability, she would be doing all the talking and making all the decisions. But after all, I was her son, and she was going to do exactly what I said. I wanted to be released, and then I would be out of that hospital, at home, and I would heal up. I felt I had been at the hospital too long already.

Heading into the meeting, I was confident that I was going home and everything was going to be all right. I had prayed, and I knew in my spirit that everything was going to go just as I had planned. I was taken to the meeting in a wheelchair. Everybody was there in the huge room when I arrived—my doctors, my therapists, my nurse, my mother, my eldest brother, and my wife.

Once I was there, everyone began to talk, one at a time, beginning with my doctors. Then my occupational therapist talked then my physical therapist, my speech therapist, and then my nurse. My family and I just sat and listened to each of them. They all started off with remarks about how much I was improving each day, which was very encouraging to me. But the reality of my situation soon escaped their mouths. They each said that although it was my choice, they all recommended that I stay in the rehabilitation ward another thirty days.

This response from them all really deflated my spirits. But then I humbly understood that my departure would not be determined by me, but by God. After the hospital staff had summarized their reports, it was my mother's turn to talk. She expressed her concerns and asked what was best for me. She thanked them for their time and patience and for working with me. Finally she concluded that she would talk with the family, and talk with me, and then give them a decision of whether I would stay or go home.

I immediately knew, when she told them that she would talk with me, that I wasn't going anywhere. I wasn't mad at her because I knew she was in charge. She was my loving mother, and I had seen her separate her emotions from her logic of what's best many times while growing up under her. I knew that she would always lead me to the right decision. In other words, she would be a mother.

How was I, the patient, feeling about everything I heard at the meeting? I must tell you, I was truly upset. I had things to do—a business to run, a church to attend, and my body had to heal up so that I could get on with my life. Even though everybody was giving his or her viewpoint on my condition and what I should do, I was ready to go home. This is just the state of mind that I was in at that moment, though I did fully trust everyone's, especially my mother's, judgment.

I was wheeled back into the private room that God had given me—I say private because there were four beds in the room, but the whole time I was in the hospital, I was the only person in the room. I tell you, God is always in control! Anyway, my mother reiterated that the final decision to stay or go would be mine, and that I had the entire weekend to make my decision, for it was Friday.

My weekend was very long. I felt that I had a decision to make, but no real choice; the decision had been made for me. If I went home, I would have to relearn how to talk and walk properly on my own, even if I did know God was there to help me. But if I stayed in the hospital, I would have the assistance of my doctors and therapists for the next thirty days, and then they would evaluate me again. But I starting thinking, what if they evaluated me in thirty days and decided I would need another thirty days? I was truly alone and scared, because this was real. This was about more than making a decision; it was also about facing my giants and their little brothers.

Well, I made the decision, and my decision was to stay at the hospital and receive the help from my doctors and from God. I decided to believe that the battle was not mine, but the Lord's. I soon realized that there were decisions in life that you have to make, that you don't want to make, but you have to make them. When I look back at my life's decisions, I believe this was the best decision that I have ever made, for it gave God a chance to show up in my life. It also allowed me the time to rest and recover from my sickness, to turn into one of God's many miracles. I guess that is why my doctor calls me the miracle man.

Chapter Five

Rehabilitation and Release

My mind spun since realizing that I would be staying an extra thirty days at the Paradise Rehabilitation Unit. This was by far the most trying time of my entire journey in life. I never knew what the next day would bring. I only knew and felt that I was in God's hands and that I had no future without him guiding me. The stresses of this life had caught up with me and had shattered me into many pieces. I was no longer in control of my path. I could no longer go any farther, and if there was a future for me, it would be because God had willed it to be so.

In the thirty days at the Paradise Rehabilitation Unit, I would get daily shots administered by the nurse. I would meet twice daily each with my physical therapist, occupational therapist, and speech therapist. The first was teaching me how to walk again, the next was teaching me how to be functional with my disability and how to become left handed, and the last was teaching me how to speak again without slurring my words. I had a challenge with this last part of my disability, because I had been called to be an evangelist, and how could I preach and save souls if I could not talk or pronounce words? This really disturbed me, for preaching was the greatest gift and greatest blessing that God had given me, and it was now gone. My constant dread was not that I would never talk again or walk again, but that would I never preach the wonderful Gospel of our Lord and Savior Jesus Christ again.

I would also see my doctors each day. This is when one of them started calling me the miracle man. I had no idea or understanding of why he was calling me that, for I did not know then as I know today that I am one of God's miracles. I am here to tell you that if He would do it for me, He will do it for you or your loved ones.

The routine went on for thirty days. When I was not with the medical staff I was in the presence of the Holy Spirit and with God in my daily thoughts. I remember one day that I was so quiet that one of the therapists sent for a psychiatrist because she thought I was deeply depressed. I was the exact opposite! I was experiencing the calmness of God, that peace that comes over you in times when everything is wrong and out of order.

When the psychiatrist came to my room, I was lying in my bed, and he asked me if I was depressed about what had occurred in my life. I told him that I was meditating on how good God had been to me and that some days I was quiet because I was listening to the direction that God was giving me. This blew him away, for I could tell by his reaction that he had never met anyone like me. He had never seen the glory of God up close, nor one of God's miracles. I believe that God allowed me to meet this person that He might get the glory into this person's life, which took place from my hospital bed. I knew that this was not my will, but it was God's will for my life. That is the way my life went for those thirty days. I was walking by faith—real faith—and not by sight.

Many days came and went since my awakening from my coma in the ICU room. My thoughts were many, and my days were long. My dominant thoughts were of going home, my business, and my future, but I knew that it did not matter what I thought or felt and that I was not in control of this situation. I could only wait on the Lord and my release from the hospital. Still, I couldn't help but wonder when I was going home and what would become of me.

One day my nurse informed me that my thirty days were coming to an end and that my next review would be coming up soon. I found out that I could be released from the hospital, or I could be retained longer for more rehabilitation if my therapists, doctors, and nurses felt it was necessary. This possibility brought fear into my heart. However, I knew that my job was to remain positive. As long as I had faith and an internal assurance that something good was going to come out of this situation, I felt that things would somehow work out to my favor. For after all, I was still alive, which meant that God was not through with me. I also knew that this was not the end of my life, but only the beginning.

What was I experiencing? I believe that my experience was tied to my perception. Why do I believe this? Because my perception was only disbelief. What I was seeing and feeling was not real to me and could not be real to me. The reality of my situation and my inner spirit were not matching up, so I felt this could not be real—the circumstances I was facing and feeling just did not seem real to me. My inner spirit was telling me that my faith would make me whole and that there was a lesson I was to learn in this process. It also was telling me to trust God and God only, for this battle was not mine alone, and this part of my life would give God glory.

What did I see? I saw that I was placed in a private room. This was a large room. Its occupancy was four people, it had four beds, yet I was in this room by myself. The blessings of God sure are good. While I would practice walking with my therapist, I would notice that the other rooms were quite small and housed two people. My belief is that even when we are experiencing our roughest times, God is there with us and giving us first-class treatment. Even if we are so caught up in our experience that we cannot see Him, He is there.

One of my therapists and my nurse had informed me that I had a weekend pass and that I would be going home that weekend. This excited me greatly; it was finally happening—I was actually going home! It did not matter if I would be there only through the weekend. It was enough just knowing that I would be there with my family and my dog—oh yes; I do love my dog, who happens to be one of my best blessings in life. To me it feels like the animals that God created seem to understand all things, even though they cannot talk. I would have many talks with my dog, and I was always right, and he never said I was wrong. So when the freedom to go home for the weekend was granted, I was very excited about getting away from the hospital, even if just for a little while.

I remember being like a child on Christmas morning. I would get a chance to stay at the place I had spent my life creating with the efforts of my talents and the goals that I had accomplished. To you this might not seem like such a big deal, but to me it was everything. The saying is true: "You don't know what you've got until it is gone."

While I was riding to my house, I noticed that even though the vehicle was going only forty miles per hour, it felt to me as if it was traveling at one hundred miles per hour. This was because my equilibrium had been affected by my stroke. I had no balance at all, and what most people do automatically, I was now doing manually, meaning to stay balanced I had to actually think about it and will it to happen. I had lost all memory of how to function on this plane, as well as how to do certain things. It was like I had lost all memory of some of the most basic functions of life; it had all been erased, and everything I had known was now blank. The mind works like a computer, I found. It has all these files containing information and coding of how to do certain functions, and if they are erased, new files must be created to carry out those functions. My ability to speak, to walk, to use my right arm—and I used to be right handed—or my right side were gone, and God had to create new files for me. I think He had to rewire me also, but that is another story.

Upon reaching home, we drove up to the sidewalk. I exited the vehicle and was placed in my wheelchair. I was restricted to a wheelchair due to my equilibrium challenges, and I could not walk at that time. While I was being strolled up the sidewalk, my dog came up to see who I was, because he did not recognize me. He had not seen me for some time now. He sniffed me with his nose to get my scent and soon realized who I was, his friend. It struck me that things had really changed; even my dog had not recognized me in my new state.

I was taken into the house, and my weekend visit began. I took in my surroundings, my home, and I began to reminisce about the good and bad times I'd had in each of the rooms. Gladness was in my heart just being in my own comfort zone and not the hospital environment. Even though I was at home, though, it felt different to me; I guess things had really changed in my life.

My weekend visit came to an end very quickly, and I was humbled by how much I had experienced and felt in this short part of my life. Even though I had slept in my own bed, eaten at my own table, and watched my own television, I felt in my heart that something had changed. I could not put a name or a feeling to it, but something was going on within me. I soon realized that what I was experiencing was happening on the inside of me. It was not the weekend visit or the family or the dog, nor was it the friends that I saw, for they were the same and nothing had changed on their insides or their outsides.

Then what was happening to me? I had changed, and I had changed in a very short time. I knew that the change was inside of me. What I did not know was if I could accept it, for it was so new to me. Yet it was so permanent. The lifestyle that I had lived was over, but I did not know exactly how this change would affect me or how it would affect others in my life—for the change did affect others also. I would soon discover the change that was to come. Whatever it was, I knew it would change my future and the futures of all those around me, I also felt that the change was very real, and that my life, would never be as it was. A season had ended and a new season had begun.

My home visit ended, and I was taken back to the hospital. It was a trip that I was ready to take, I guess; visiting my home during this time was too much for me. I found that I missed the comfort of the hospital, my nurses, my therapists, and my doctors, for they were there to help me and comfort me. At home and having to depend on myself, I must confess, was something I was not ready for. I just wasn't yet up to facing head-on the people, my dog, and the challenges of life.

Now back in the comfort of the hospital, I was safe, or at least I thought so. I had many thoughts upon my mind—thoughts about my future, my business, and my health. Even though my consciousness had many thoughts running through it, I knew that God would take care of everything and direct my path, wherever it was to lead. I knew that my God could do anything and everything and that He was able to meet my needs and much more. So my trust, my faith, my reliance, and my confidence were once again placed in God.

I was lying in my bed one day at the hospital having a pity party by myself. As I lay there, the Holy Spirit spoke to me. I don't know if you have met the Holy Spirit, but I will tell you He does exist. I believe that He was reintroducing Himself to me. I had heard this voice when I had been called to the ministry and when I had been directed to carry out the purpose of my life—to serve God. At times in my life the voice had spoken to me when I was so busy with my own pursuits that I was not listening to the heeding of His Word, which I should have, but God has forgiven me for these times in my life.

The Holy Spirit had me right where He wanted me, in the hospital bed. I could not move or talk, I could only listen. He called me by my first name, Ronnie. He knows everyone's name and all about us, and He is with us ever since we have accepted Christ into our lives.

The voice said two things to me. First He addressed my having a pity party. He asked me why I was beating up on myself and why I was getting so depressed about this situation. I responded by saying, "Look at me. I can't talk, I can't walk, I can't use my right side—I can't do anything." I went on and on about how I couldn't do this or why I couldn't I do that.

The voice waited until I got through complaining about my dilemma, and He said these words to me: "Ronnie, don't you know that the spirit of God cannot have a stroke, nor can it be sick, nor can it catch the flu?"

In that very moment time stood still and I realized that the physical body could be affected, but the spiritual body could never be sick or die. I also realized in that moment that my physical body had been affected, but my spiritual body was alive and well. In fact, it had only grown and been strengthened by God. I again knew then that everything would be all right; it was only a matter of time, and this was but one season of my life.

The second thing the voice told me was, "Ronnie, you will be leaving San Diego, California, and going to Tacoma, Washington, to recover from your illness."

I listened to the voice, but I did not understand this message, nor did I want to hear it. I did not understand or want to understand because what I *did* understand was that moving to another state would mean closing up all of my businesses, leaving my home church, and changing my entire lifestyle and all that I knew. And did this decision include only me? What about my wife, who was suffering from an enlarged heart and who was also beginning to have kidney problems, for which she was undergoing treatments? And what about my ministry?

I felt that I had plenty of reasons not to listen to this voice. I felt that it was Satan, and I could easily blame the voice on Satan, but I knew that in my heart that it was God and that I was to obey and heed His Word. What helped me was when the Spirit told me that I would probably die if I stayed in San Diego, for I needed rest that I could only get by leaving San Diego. Going to Tacoma would allow me to get the rest and the healing that I would need, and the voice assured me that God would talk and walk with me.

This was a big decision for me; in fact, it was the biggest decision that I had ever made. I kept what I knew and heard from the Holy Spirit to myself, for I felt that if I did not understand, how could anyone else understand? It was something that I could not talk about to anyone without them thinking that I had lost my mind or that it was my illness talking. I knew this was one of those decisions that one doesn't want to make, but one has to make anyway.

My review board had been scheduled to take place. I would go through the same thing that I had gone through in the first week of my stay. The board of my caretakers and family would meet and decide if I needed another thirty days in the rehabilitation ward. I was not feeling as much anxiety as I had before, because I felt in my heart that I knew the answer that the board would give. I would be released from the hospital. I knew this because I had prayed, and I had faith that I would be released. Plus, the Holy Spirit had told me to go to Washington to recover.

The day of the review came, and all the various people were there to give their reports. My mom, wife, my brother Karl, nurses, doctors, and therapists were all in attendance. After listening to each of the staff's reports on my progress, a decision for my release was made, and a date for me to leave the hospital and go home was fixed. I was glad about being released from the hospital, but at the same time I was burdened. I knew that my journey would be taking on a new direction, and everything that I knew was going to change.

Chapter Six

Breaking the News

This journey that I have been on since my stroke has been some type of ride. It has been different from life before in many ways, yet I do believe that I have gained wisdom in some areas. I'd also experienced pure confusion in some other areas; the nights and the days were all the same to me, but I must say that God was in the midst of all of it. Now I was finally going home after more than a month in the hospital. The time had finally arrived.

I didn't know if I was ready yet to experience the joy of being at my home, versus living at the hospital. It was the first week of November. I had seen a small glimpse of what it would be like at the house when I had visited for a weekend. It had not been what I'd expected. The nurses were not there to look after me. It was quite a shock to me, especially how I had gotten used to the nurses. But now I was headed home, not knowing, what I would experience there. I only had God and my thoughts, but I was not afraid. I was rather calm not knowing what my future held. God had delivered my soul, His presence, and His peace into my life. I did not know what was in front of me, but I was willing to accept by faith and His Grace what I was to come upon in my life.

I was hopefully never to return to the hospital until it was truly time for me to return. My reports from the doctors, nurses, and therapists had all came back positive. I would like to say that I have a great appreciation for the hospital staff and the work that they did for me. Without them diligently working and caring for me when I really needed someone to not only pray for me but to care for me and smile at me, I probably would not be around today. Thank God for the hospital staff.

The day of my release was a good day. I have seen many days, but I had finally realized that I was not in control. It is only our belief, as humans that we are in control, until we hit the ground or fall off the wall and get a good dose of reality. Now upon my release, I was at peace with myself and with what I had experienced. It had become my past, and only my future was now on my path, and I would face it with faith.

The only thing I was facing—and it was heartbreaking—was that I would have to break the news to my wife, Brendolyn, that I was moving to Washington, and without her. This was the worst conversation to have with my mate that I could think of, and I was dreading to have it. I wondered how God could request me to do this. You are probably wondering, how I explained my moving to Washington to Brendolyn, This is what I said. Brendolyn, I will be moving to Washington State, so that I might recover from this illness, and then I will either come and get you, or come back here, when it is time, and that I believe God has told me to do this, or I will die. She responded by saying, Ronnie you know that I don't get into God's business. That was Brendolyn's answer. She always trusted me and trusted God, in all situations. The rest of our conversation, I would like to keep to myself. I do want you to know that we made the decision together, for me to move to Washington for my recovery. I felt that my absence would be only for a short time and that God would make a way, somehow, for us to be back together as one person, in some way. It was one of those decisions that you have to make that you don't want to make. But I was going to trust God with my life and move to Washington.

Dear reader, this part of my journey was very heartbreaking for me and Brendolyn. That is the reason, that it is the shortest chapter of, "the Awakening" Even though I would catch a train from Washington to San Diego, each month to be with Brendolyn, my thoughts and dreams of her, where only living nightmares to me. I don't know, if I had shared this with you, she was not only a heart patient, but also was suffering from Kinney failure, so she could not make this trip with me, we could only depend on God and His direction for our lives. Even, if it meant being away from each other for a short while.

Chapter Seven

Washington

This chapter is on the direction I took after leaving the hospital—my healing process, my life while in Washington during my recovery, and my life now, as it is today. When we are directed by God to do something, we must listen to what He says, and that is what I did. It does not matter how foreign His Word sounds, for it truly sounds foreign, but we must listen to the voice regardless. The voice is never wrong, but man is often wrong when he listens to himself. When man follows the direction given him by the voice, he is often led to his destiny and the true purpose of his life.

While lying in my hospital bed in San Diego, trying to figure out in my mind and heart what I should do, there were many thoughts upon my mind. I was thinking about who would run my business during my recovery, how I would pay my bills, and what would I do to survive. I had worked twenty years, in establishing my business, I had set short term and long term goals, I had read all the inspirational books, and yet I had reached a place, that had no answers, to my many thoughts, to think of my present state of being or to think of my future being, only created within me, more and more fear, of the unknown. I could only go within myself and listen to the voice that was within me. I knew within my heart that I must trust the voice that was within me, for it had given me clear direction on the path, that I should take, and that I should listen to the voice, no matter how foreign or disturbing it sounded to me. I decided to follow the voice and let the voice provide the leadership, the direction and the control of my life.

And so the journey began. I was on my way to Washington.

Through my rehab, I had gained a small victory with my speech. I could now talk, but I still slurred every word. I did not have any voice pitch; I had to try to control it manually with much thought. I was not quite perfect.

What do I mean by that? We are born and created in God's image, in our natural state. We are, as far as God is concerned, perfect in his creation process, in his image. It is at this moment of creation when our souls are connected and created in his hands, so we are perfect in his eyesight, as far as nature is concerned. Over our lives, we strive to perfect what is already perfect as we go through the metamorphism process in our soul's development. This is when our souls are connected to our natural bodies; perfection is in progress, and our wholeness forming.

When we are born, everything works. We don't even think about what we are doing. Our mind thinks on its own, our heart pumps on its own, never missing a beat, our lungs breathe fresh air without any assistance, our eyes see the beautiful images of this world. Our legs cannot only walk, once we learn, but they can also run. Our arms can reach, they can lift, and they can stretch. Without thinking about how to do it, our hands can write, once we learn, and they can pick up things. Our bodies can do much more than this—our internal parts can do things without our assistance, as well. We are born on automatic pilot, and we grow into perfection.

My point is this! I was not on automatic pilot anymore. I was on manual. My internal parts had shut off and rebooted themselves. They needed to reprogram themselves; parts of me, I believe, I had to be rewired because of the stroke. All creation has a stimulus, pause, and a response. For instance, you could cut yourself, which is your stimulus, then you would look at the wound, that is your pause, and then you would either yell for help or bandage the wound, which is your response. All humans have this order of reflexes.

Well guess what? I had developed a stimulus, pause, pause, response order of things. I could cut myself and not even know it unless I just happened to notice it because my right side was totally numb at all times. I had taught myself how to stand up and walk on a cane with the help of my physical therapist during my hospital stay, but I walked with a drag, meaning that my legs were walking out of balance. My right arm and hand were still paralyzed, which was quite a challenge for me, having been right handed before. The thought of losing so much ability really frightened me.

My journey to Washington was by highway, for my equilibrium would not tolerate air travel. It made me very nervous. I had never been nervous of any form of travel, but things had changed for me. I did not know what to expect; this was a trip that I was not too excited about. Why did God want me to go to Tacoma, Washington? The good news is that my eldest brother, Karl, lived there, and I would be able to stay with him for a little while. There were many challenges before me that I had to face, whether it was in San Diego or elsewhere. I did wonder if the voice that I'd heard within, at the hospital, was real. When I arrived in the strange town and saw it with my natural eyes, I felt that this could not be where God wanted me to be. I was like a duck out of water.

Do you believe in Angels? Well I always have, even though I had never seen one until my stay in the hospital, when I thought I saw two during my coma. My belief is centered in the Word of God. The Word always makes parallels—Heaven and Earth, Heaven and Hell, Angels and Demons—you can go on and on. So if the Bible said there are Angels, that's good enough for me. I believe that if an Angel showed themselves to a human, the man or woman would probably have a heart attack due to the glory, the angelic presence, and the angelic majesty of the angelic being. The Angel would have to present itself in another form, that we may behold its presence. This is probably why the Word says, "Angels come unaware." There are books written on this subject, but this is not one of them.

But, why all this fuss about Angels? Well, I believe God sent me one to watch after me, should I dash my foot against a stone. Well, I had certainly dashed my foot against a stone, and there was room in my life for an Angel. As a matter of fact, there was room for a miracle, and I needed one, badly. I needed one so badly that God sent me one, even though I didn't know it then, as I do now.

Let me try to explain. I believe that no matter what you are going through, God knows about it and has provided the necessary provisions, care and love, that you will need to make it through. The Word declares this, and I believe it, for it happened for me. I will take a moment and say, isn't God good? God had placed an Angel in my life, even though I didn't recognize it until much later.

I knew the Angel before my health problems began, but I never knew the part the Angel would play in my future. Let me explain the term Angel as I see it. I believe that God has so place different people in our lives, even though we don't see them for what they, and who they are, until a crisis, emerges in our lives. They are not six feet tall or taller, nor do they have a set of wings, and they are people, with the divinity of God within themselves. They are fearless, and they do have the ability, to see only your needs and not there owns, at the time of your need, and can be of great service to you, and they do all this free of charge, for they are design to do so. I never knew that when the darkness would consume my life and my world that the Angel, would appear and take charge of my journey. You don't know or recognize their importance in your life, until they are to act in your life, it is in their design to be there for you, when you, really need them to be there for you. My Angel was there to take care of me and provide me with protection and kindness, even when there was no kindness or love within me—only pity and despair, confusion and fear of tomorrow. Do you wonder what is in the minds of the sick? Well, I will tell you. Fear is in their minds, for they feel they have no tomorrow.

As I said, that Angel drove me from California to Washington. I had no one else to help me. I could not drive myself, I could not talk, and I could not walk, but God had a purpose for my life, as he has one for yours. The Angel stayed in my life for about two years, until

I was able to talk and provide for myself. I still see the Angel from time to time, but just like it appears in my life now and again at times, it leaves for times.

I arrived at Karl's house—my big brother. He has always been very special to me. He has always looked after me and protected me; this is the way our mother brought us up. Remember, her favorite saying for our family is, "All we have is one another." My natural family has always believed this and lived by it. I must say this to you about Karl. Karl is my mother's first born child. He was always the protector of our family, and he was all ways the one, with the greatest amount of pressure as well as stress upon him. My mother all ways had to depend on him, to watch over us, as well as to raise the younger children in the family. He has always been my hero, and I wanted to grow up and be just like him. He is special and the world is a better place because of him. I knew in my heart, even though I would bring him much trouble, popping up out of know where, meaning that he did not know when I was coming, but he expected me, for he was my big brother. I knew that he would take care of me and fight my battles, for me and with me, because we had been raised that way by my mother, to always look after one another.

I was glad to arrive at my brother's house, but soon I realized that it would not be easy for me. Why? Because many years had passed since my brother and I had been in the same place. Even though he had been baptized and knew Jesus, the pressures of this life had worn on his soul, and he and his wife had drinking problems. They were alcoholics. At this time they were also having trouble in their marriage, as we all do. The two sons that God had blessed them with were not honoring their parents or God. I was in a bad place, for I already had big giants in my life, and here were more giants to fight.

But I knew that prayer worked, and I was a praying man. I was trying to find my complete healing, I was trying to find God, and I was trying to find the light at the end of the tunnel. I soon realized that this was where all that was going to happen, whether I liked it or not. I must say that I never liked that time at my brothers' house at all, for I was used to having my own house and being independent in all facets of my life, including my belief in God. I guess I felt forsaken and confused with what I was seeing and feeling and needing. I needed healing—not tomorrow, but today, in my present, so I was very angry about coming to Washington. Nevertheless, I kept telling myself that God had plans for me, so I got my ego out the way and just followed Him with my life.

Washington was very different from California. I really missed my church at home. I had been a part of that church for over twenty years, even though I would go to various other churches from time to time. Yet surely Dorothy had it right when she said, "There's no place like home."

I endured every day of my existence in Washington, trying to fit not only in my new surroundings, but also in my brother's life. I know that I was beginning, after a while, to be a burden upon him and his wife's nerves, for all I talked about was the Word. They never understood that that was all I had and all I could hold on to in my life. I knew that my life, my healing, my future, my prosperity, and my wellbeing were in the promises of God. I was at a point in my life when I was being put back together after having been shattered. Even though I wanted to be on my own, it was not time, and I would have to learn patience—something I thought I had but soon found I was lacking. There are many levels of patience. I will tell you a great secret. The hardest thing to do in the world, when you are used to being productive and goal oriented, is nothing. And that is about all that I could do for the time being.

Now, the injuries to my physical body were many, but I didn't fully know it. I trusted so much in God's blessing and healing that I never paid much attention to my aliments or my condition. Even though I was taking all kinds of medications and going to see speech, physical, and occupational therapists, I did not pay much heed to it all. Even though I had all this darkness in my life, I still believed in my heart and soul that I was healed. The Word said that I was healed, and that's all I needed to hear.

I believed that my doctors had given up on me, based on their medical reports, which was quite depressing. It's a wonder why so many people are depressed, when they should be happy and smiling, enjoying this gift of life. The doctors felt that I should not be alive at all, but I knew the promises of God, and I also knew that my work was not finished, for God had told me so while I was in the coma. I was one of God's miracles.

While I stayed with my brother Karl, I would spend the most of my time, reading my Bible and seeing and meeting, Doctors and Nurses, that had been assign to me, to help in my rehabilitation. I would often believe that my healing would come; that day and that everything would go back to normal, but it never came. I had to learn to listen to God daily, and accept his will for my life. The day came when I could finally move to my own dwelling. It was not far from my brother's house. I must say that it was long overdue, but God did not let me down. It was a three-bedroom home with a double garage for my car and truck, which I had had brought up to Washington from California, even though I could not drive at the time. I was finally in my own place, where God's blessing would take place in my life. It goes to say that it does not matter where you live; God can bless you right where you are. He was late, but He was on time. I truly knew what that meant. I felt happy, blessed, and favored.

I was grateful to be in my own house. I had a kitchen, a living room, a dining room, a family room, a fireplace, a front yard, a backyard, and even a driveway. I say I was happy, but one thing about me did make me miserable. When I looked in the mirror, I did not recognize this new Ronnie. Before, I had been 140 pounds, and now I was 230 pounds—I was overweight and getting bigger. The weight came from sitting on the couch and watching television because I could not walk or run. I was truly at the mercy of what I was eating and what I was doing to myself. I decided that I should join a gym before I was three hundred pounds, from lack of exercise and movement. I was truly a mess, physically. I could still barely talk, I still could not walk without a cane, I was overweight, and of course I had no use of my right side. So despite the new house, I was miserable.

But I had enough faith in myself to know that this was not the person that God had created and that I should not be satisfied with this person, whoever it was. All I knew was it was not me. I joined a gym, though I believe that they were afraid to give me a membership because they probably felt that I was one step from death and was afraid that if it happened at their gym, they would get sued. But by the grace of God, they gave me a membership.

I want to stop right here and tell you that whoever you are, whatever physical aliment is stopping you from receiving your healing—if you are overweight, depressed, or have given up on your condition—hear me well: exercise can help you. I will say that again: exercise can help you! It performed miracles for me. Now, understand that the transformation does not happen overnight, but it happens, and you will then have the quality of life that you deserve. It took me five years of going to the gym, five days a week.

This is what I did. First, I learned to eat the right foods. Also, I pulled away from my dinner table and began to eat in proper portions, but most of all I ate the right foods. If you eat the right foods, you can eat as much as you want, but the great success you have from proper exercise and proper eating will make you eat less and also enjoy your life more.

Secondly, find the exercise that fits you. For me it was a treadmill. I could not lift weights or use any piece of equipment in the gym but the treadmill, and I would hold onto it for dear life because I had no balance and could not walk correctly and I was 230 pounds. But I learned to get up on it and stay on it. At first it scared me to death, but my desire to change was greater than my desire to stay the same. I set a goal, limp leg and all, to get on this treadmill for fifteen minutes a day, and that is what I did. Those fifteen minutes gave me new life, but most importantly, I lost fifty pounds on that treadmill and by eating the proper foods. It gave me what I needed, and that is confidence—the confidence to be me, to be what God had created, to have a life beyond the couch, to have a future, and to see the light in my life.

Over time, the fifteen minutes on the treadmill expanded into thirty minutes, and then forty-five minutes, and eventually to one hour. The healing began to happen. My limp leg was moving, and somehow it began to correct itself. My balance began to come back. I began to lift weights with the right side of my body. It was truly a blessing. This magic, or should I say healing, can happen to you also, if you learn to believe in yourself and in your healing, for your destiny is in front of you, and your sickness will take you to that destiny.

The next part of my journey was good, but it was also bad. I had decided that it was time to get my life back in order. I wanted more from my life, and I knew it was not over, so I decided to go back to college. My body was impaired, but my mind had been reorganized and my spirits were high. I once again knew that my future was in front of me. I enrolled in Tacoma Community College and began to study law. I did not want to become a lawyer, but they had an excellent paralegal program. I did not know why I was I being directed this way. I must tell you I was afraid; I had already been to college. Despite these things, I gathered up my strength and newfound confidence in myself and enrolled anyway.

After about a year of going to this college, it began to snow one day. Yes, I said snow, in Seattle! It looked so white and beautiful that I just had to go out in it and build a snowman. I went out in the snow with my boots on, but I left my cane in the house. Guess what happened—I slipped and fell and broke my foot! This was the bad part of this segment of my journey, and I knew it. It meant no school, no treadmill, and no walking. I was devastated; I had come so far.

There was more goodness to come, even though I did not know it. For now all I knew was that I had broken my foot in half. The doctors would not even do surgery, for they told me that it was a clean break and that it would have to heal naturally. Now I had a decision to make about school, and it would require a lot of faith. I had only done one year, and I was looking at another year before graduating. I did not want to wait a possible six months to heal, which meant leaving school. So I decided, and it took a lot of faith, to go to school just as I was, broken foot and all.

I would have to go about in a wheelchair. I had already been in a wheelchair, right after the stroke, and I wanted no part of it again. But sometimes in life, you have to make decisions that you really don't want to make. And so I went back to school to finish my schooling, wheelchair and all. The decision to go on through school astonished my teachers and fellow students, and I am sure it gave them inspiration and informed them that I was determined and special. But I knew in my heart that God makes a way out of no way.

Here is the remaining good news. Because of the stroke, my right foot had become a peg foot, which means that it was flat. It would not operate as a normal foot would.

This event puzzles me to this day. Had God done this? If so why? But in any case, when my break mended back together, my foot was no longer flat. I could actually walk on it normally again! Isn't God good? Through this process, He gave me back my right foot, and I am now walking just like you. Praise God!

Well I must tell you that the bad parts of this season of my life were not over. I was about three months from graduating paralegal school. I had a lot of confidence in myself, for I knew that even though I had disabilities and was slow in healing, I had a new awakening to this life. My life was going to be better than ever, for I was now walking even closer with God than before.

Then I suffered another setback. In my home, the bedrooms were upstairs, with the staircase being in an L shape. I used one of the bedrooms as a study and computer room. My computer had run out of space, so I decided I would go the computer store and have more storage put in it, which would be cheaper than buying a new computer.

I figured all I had to do was take the computer down the stairs, through the hallway, into the garage, and put it into my truck. Simple right? At least that's what I thought. I carried the computer out of the room and I went to the stairs, trying to be very careful. But then, for some reason, my foot missed a step near the top of the stairs. I became airborne, and it was like the quiet before the storm. Time slowed down. I knew I was falling. I remember calling on Jesus, in midair, for I was helpless. I was now at God's mercy.

I passed out on the way down. When I woke up at the bottom of the first level of the stairs, there was a big hole in the wall. The computer was lying beside me broken, for I had let it go while falling. The wall that I'd put a hole in had prevented me from tumbling all the way into my living room. Now I was awake, but something was wrong. I could not raise my right arm. It was crooked, and I figured it was broken. All of my physical strength was gone, as if my natural body had been transported someplace else during this time after I had called on the name of Jesus during my fall.

Let us continue. Because I called on Jesus while falling, I didn't feel the fall or the damage to my arm. But I sure felt when I woke up and knew the arm was broken. I managed to crawl to the couch, but I knew I needed some help. I always kept my cell phone in my pocket, and I called for help. I was able to reach my Angel, who has always been there when I needed help. God is always there when you need help. It is a reason that the 23rd Psalms declares, that surely goodness and mercy, shall follow you, all the days of your life, as you dwell in the "House" of the Lord.. I was taken to the hospital. After many hours of waiting for a report, I was informed that I had shattered my elbow and broken my wrist and that this was ranked as the third worst break that the hospital had ever had. They told me that I would need surgery, and that the surgery would take eight hours. Yeah—eight hours!

This devastated me. I had finally gotten my foot acting right, I was no longer in a wheelchair, and I was just three months from graduating paralegal school. What was I supposed to do? Why was I having all this trouble? What had I done wrong in my life to deserve this? Many negative thoughts went through my mind again and again. But let me share this with you. I believe that if you have a purpose to fulfill in your life, you will come up against all types of opposition—or should I say pure evil, even—that will try to prevent you from fulfilling that purpose.

After my surgery, my elbow had been reconstructed and was now metal. My wrist was operated on also, because it required metal in order for it to heal and function correctly. I had truly become the bionic man on my right side, what with the pains and everything in my partially healed broken foot, and now an arm full of metal.

Believe it or not, I had been through so much during this season of my life that I came to think that it really did not matter. I had long ago learned to put my faith and life in the healing process of God. What bothered me was, how was I going to finish school with three months remaining? Was I going to drop out and finish after I healed, or was I going to go ahead and graduate on schedule? You guessed it—I went back to school after missing just a week out of school, as medicated as I could be, in an elbow and wrist cast. It was a sight to see. I was determined that nothing was going to stop me from completing my purpose in this life—no one would stop me from being who I was and becoming what I was becoming. I was going to persevere through the opposition and evil.

When I finally arrived home after the hospital stay, I saw where I fell from and the big hole in the wall, and I must tell you, I should have broken my neck. This was truly another time in my life that God had prevented me from dying. It is by His grace that I am still around to share this part of my life with you. Let me stop right here and say some words of encouragement before I continue: I am sharing these episodes of my journey because I want you to know that *your* life's journey is not going to be perfect. There will be bad times, and you will have good times, as well. You will survive those bad times. One thing you will be able to hold on to is that all things—I mean *all* things, whether good or bad—will work out for good, because favor surrounds each and every one of our life's journeys. No matter what it looks or feels like at any one point in time, you will be victorious in your efforts if you live your life righteously. The circumstances and the conditions that you will experience will not matter if you have God's protection. You will make it to the next stage of your journey, whatever shape it takes or forms..

I would like to conclude, this chapter by saying to you, never, never, give up! No matter what you go through, you have a purpose for living. I could never tell you everything that has happened to me here in Washington, but hope that these events encourage you and help you to defeat all the bad circumstances and conditions in your life. Awaken now, and live this life, and never go back to sleep.

Chapter Eight

Seasons

For everything there is a season—a time for everything to start and to finish. Life truly comes in seasons. One minute the sun is shining in our lives. The next minute the rain is pouring in our lives. This is the summer season in our life. Before we know it, we are experiencing the fall of our lives. I think that season is a thinking time, when we decide what direction to take in life. And finally, we have winter in our lives. It is snowy or rainy, cold, and miserable. This is a period when we stand still on our paths until the bright sunshine comes into our lives. That is the spring of our lives, when we are happy, confident, and driven to accomplish whatever dreams that we have.

At that moment, the seasons start all over again. This has been the case throughout my journey and my life.

Many things happened on my journey since I graduated paralegal school and made my recovery from that fall down the stairs. On January 6, 2008, my wife, who this book is dedicated to, went on to be with the Lord. After thirty-two years of marriage and many obstacles conquered, dreams created, and goals to achieved, she went on to be with her creator. Am I sad? Yes, of course I'm sad. But I'm also happy—happy for her, because I know that God has other work for her to do in Heaven. He had just let me borrow her for a little while, for she belonged to Him all along.

With the conclusion of this book, I would like to keep a promise that I made to my wife Bren. I promised that I would tell her story. Bren's death was devastating to me, for I truly lost my greatest friend here on earth. It has affected me greatly. She always encouraged me on my journey—to go back to school when I did not want to go back, to go on various missionary trips, and more. It is different now for me without her. It is true that you never miss what you have until it is gone.

Whenever I think of Canada, I often think of Bren. It was in Canada when she gave her life to Christ. I watched her walk into glory to give her life to Christ, and when she came back from receiving Christ as her personal savior, I saw a glow upon her face. Our lives were never the same; I had received my mate from God.

How my life is now? The only answer I can give you is that it is different, much different. But we all must have times and seasons that stretch out before us.

Before going any further, I would like to share with you that this is a true story as well as a love story. Also, the story is still ongoing today, for life is only a transition from one world into another world.

Bren, as her family and friends affectionately called her, first crossed my path when I was twenty-two years of age. I cannot share every detail of all thirty-two years of our relationship together, but I will share some of the most important times that we experienced together. When I first saw Bren, I was with a friend of mine in San Diego, California. I asked him who that was, and he told me that he knew her and her name was Brenda. I asked him to introduce her to me, and he politely informed me that she did not want me.

I just looked at him. How could he fix his mouth to say such a thing to me? Especially when I was looking at the most beautiful woman that I had ever seen! I told my friend to introduce me anyway. Even though I felt I had some looks about myself, what did I have to lose? So he introduced me as his friend from his hometown, and I smiled and said my name and we soon departed. To tell you the truth, I think I was too scared to say anything else.

The next time I saw Bren, I was by myself, so I figured that this was my chance to properly introduce myself. I went up to her and said, "How are you? Do you remember me?"

She said, "Yes, I do remember you; you were with my friend James, and you are from his hometown." Almost before she could finish that last sentence, she said to me, "I was just being nice to you because you were with my friend, but you need to know I have a man, and you should get out of my face."

I did not know what to say. I had no answer for this statement, and I had no answer for her. She just waited there for an answer, but I had none. I politely turned around, like a dog with his tail between his legs, and departed gracefully. I must admit that even as I walked away, I knew I did like this girl. I had never had any problems with the opposite sex, and I had always had a quick response. But with this woman, I had finally met my match, so I hadn't said anything; I just walked away silently. I did not know what I could say.

I did not see Bren again for six months. There had been a change in my life, and I had really taken an emotional bruising. During that span, my younger sister had died. I could not understand how God could take a seventeen-year-old. My great-grandmother had died when I was younger, but she was 103 years of age. This death was different, and it tore my whole world apart. I had never experienced such a thing so close to me. It truly did affect my reality and my life's course. I had many questions that no one could answer, but we had a closed-casket memorial service, which did not help me one bit.

How did I handle this? I blamed God. How could God let this happen? What was the purpose of this death? I watched my mother change into another person that week. The structure of my family was shattered into many pieces. I gave up on God and all that He represented.

I was miserable, confused, and lost. I felt that I had no friends and that God did not care about anybody; in fact, there must not be a God. I had all the evidence that I needed to back up my beliefs. And I didn't care if I was wrong about Him, for I wanted nothing to do with Him or His Son.

What does all this have to do with Bren? Six months later, I met Bren again, the lady who would become my wife. It was proof of how divine acts of God happen in our lives. I was walking in downtown San Diego, minding my own business. I was in the Navy, and in between my shifts and my job, I would leave the ship and enter the civilian world. As I looked forward in my path, there was Bren. Our last encounter was fresh in my mind. Quite frankly, she scared me speechless. I remembered how politely she had told me to get out of her face, and I remembered so vividly because I had never met anyone like her—someone who had made a judgment decision about me in a matter of moments.

So here she was again, and I faced the question of what would I say. Should I say anything at all, or should I just walk by and say nothing? As she got closer, I mustered up enough confidence to say, "Hello, how are you doing? Don't you remember me?"

She looked at me and said, "Yes I remember you, and don't you remember what I told you before?"

I didn't know that she had a great gift of remembering things and events—especially numbers, which I would find out later. Anyway, what Bren did not know was what had occurred in my life in the past six months and that I no longer cared about anybody at that time. I said to her in as polite a tone as I could, "Lady I didn't ask you about all of that. I just asked you how you were doing." And then I shut up.

She looked at me with a cold look, eyes that said, "No he didn't just say that." She only smiled at me and said, "I am doing fine."

I politely said, "Good," and went about my business.

I saw Bren again about three days later. She smiled at me and talked to me like I was a friend, telling me that I had a bad temper. From that day on, we were inseparable, and we became boyfriend and girlfriend.

That is the story of how we met, and I share this with you for one reason: if you have someone special in your life, you had better love them *now* like you have never loved anyone, because you only have them for a little while. God has only loaned them to you for a short time, and you must one day return them to their creator.

If you have been reading since the beginning of this book, you know that I have had many seasons in my life. I hope that this will be your awakening to your life and your true destiny. I shared with you, in the above paragraphs, about Brenda and I and the wonderful time and seasons that we had together until she went on to glory. I feel that I will see her again when it is time to see her, and I am thankful for that. There are so many things I would like to talk about that we did not get a chance to discuss in life. You see, my beloveds, everybody has seasons, including me and her. I promised her that I would tell the world about her one day, and now I have. Thank you for allowing me to tell the story of our romance. Even though I have had many seasons, in my journey. This part of my journey was the best seasons, that I had ever experience. Now let me finish describing my journey.

> To everything there is a season and a time for every matter or purpose under Heaven: A time to be born and a time to die, a time to plant and a time to pluck up what is planted.

> A time to kill and a time to heal, a time to break down and a time to build up.
> A time to weep and a time to laugh, a time to mourn and a time to dance.
> A time to cast away stones and a time to gather stones together, a time to embrace and a time to refrain from embracing.
> A time to get and a time to lose, a time to keep and a time to cast away.
> A time to rend and a time to sew, a time to keep silence and a time to speak.
> A time to love and a time to hate, a time to war and a time for peace.
> (Ecclesiastes 3:1–9)

I mentioned that Bren went home to be with the Lord on January 6, 2008. She was truly the love of my life. God gave us thirty-two years together, and they were the most wonderful years of my life. They were some of my best seasons. The loss of Bren was a very difficult season in my life. I was getting ready to go on a mission trip to the field, specifically, India. I really didn't need anything on my mind except the Indian people, but then the death of a loved one—the woman of my life—occurred and rocked my world.

My thoughts and questions were, why me? Why was I having all of this trouble? Isn't it someone else's turn? I have to go to the field for mission; aren't I following you, Lord? Despite the many questions upon my heart, I knew that such was the way of things, so I rested in my season and knew that I needed to stay within myself and take care of the business that needed to be taken care of. That was leaving Washington, driving to San Diego, holding my wife's funeral and burial, then driving back to Washington and leaving for the mission field trip to India within a week of returning. No matter what I was feeling or what season I was in, I would have to accept in my heart that this was the season of *my* life, and no one but me could go through, or experience, or grow from the season but me.

The rest is another story that might be told one day, but this was my season to experience all the emotions and thoughts that one feels when a part of you is gone forever. I tell you, my beloved reader, if you have someone who has been with you and grown up with you and raised a family with you and stuck by you for better or worse, you had better learn to love them and hold them while you can, for someday there will be a season in *your* life that you must prepare for—and embrace—and then you'll have to go on the rest of your journey all alone. The good news is that you will make it, for your joy will come in the morning.

This is what God did for me through my aneurism and my stroke, not being able to walk, talk, or write with my right hand, having to ride in a wheelchair, and having been in a coma. All those events were seasons that I had to go through in order to accept my next and greatest season, which was Bren's death. Some seasons will bring you joy, and some will bring you pain, but you will be a better person because of each. Some time along the way you will experience your season of awakening. Isn't this better than living a boring, long, dragged-out life?If you accept your seasons, and your "awakening. You will not only be "awake," but you will also experience the journeys, that you were design to experience.

To everything there is a season, a time for every matter or purpose under Heaven. These words were written by Solomon. Some say he was the wisest man that ever lived. I know that he is right when he says *everything*. He doesn't mean just humans; he means animals, clouds, birds, and everything that is in existence in this world and the next. Everything that we think matters actually is important to us at that time, but we soon find that most things didn't matter after all, but they did have their purpose in our lives.

Solomon goes on to say that everything has a purpose—that means *everything,* for everything that happens or is conceived in our minds has a cause and an effect. The cause will create the effect in our dreams, goals, families, and plans. Our purpose is foretold by who we are and what we do with this precious gift of life. Is it our purpose just to build a fine, fancy house, only to leave it here when we die? Or to buy and ride in a fancy new car, only to leave it to someone else? Our seasons will reveal to us the truth about ourselves and the true purposes of our lives, and I will tell you, that purpose won't be to buy a new house or drive a fancy car. It is much bigger than that.

There is a time when we enter this world—through birth. We don't ask to be born, but we show up on this earth anyway. We don't know then why we are here, we are just here. The journey called life begins with each and every one of us not knowing what our futures hold. We have been born, and we will die. We enter a place that we have never been, and our works, achievements, goals, and beliefs shape our character and define the life that we lived under Heaven. We ask ourselves many questions: who are we, and what is my purpose in life? What am I supposed to do with this gift? For life is only a measurement of time, and we soon realize that it is a short time and that life is truly a vapor that comes and goes in an instant. One day that we cannot know of in advance, it is over, and then the unknown becomes our reality.

The answer to how we have lived is in our seasons. What did we do with our gift of life? Did we just have kids and more kids? Buy houses and more houses? Buy cars and more cars? What an empty life.

The answer is in our seasons. Was it a time to plant and to pluck up what has been planted? What have you planted? Love? Hate? Wealth, Envy, or Jealousy? Whatever you have planted will surely come to fruition in your season. If you have planted love, you will pluck up love. If you have planted hatred, you will truly be hated in your season. If you have planted jealousy, you will surely be jealous of others.

The best thing that you can plant is love. You will be able to plant this divine essence within your heart and mind and words, such that you may spread them to all of God's creations. The message of love—its boundaries, its heights and depths are limitless, in formulation as well as creation, for you are a creature of love. As a matter of fact, you have been created to love in this world and the next world. The seasons of your life will show you the way to true love and happiness after your birth.

Solomon says that there will be a time to kill and a time to break down and a time to build up. Does it make any sense to kill, to take some human being's life, which you did not give them? Is it right to make a conscious decision to take that individual's life, as if you created them or have the power to make that decision, just because you have hatred or bitterness or even jealousy in your heart? I tell you, my brother or sister, if you think so, you are walking and living in darkness, and you are following the dark thoughts of your imagination. You are also not living up to the being that created you. Do you think in your wildest thoughts that God created you so your total purpose was and is to take another life?

Well, in case no one else has told you, you were made by the creator in His image and for His purposes and not your own. Under that layer of hatred and darkness there dwells love. Love for your brother and sister, and love for your creator. And you are precious in His sight. There is a time to be healed from all the disappointments that you have had because of things in this world. Who has you thinking that you have to defend for yourself, provide for yourself, protect yourself from the jealousy of another because you think they have something that belongs to you—because you have not had the breaks that they have had? There is time to be healed in your mind and to awaken to the true nature that dwells within you, if you would only believe in He who has formed you.

I know you might say, "How do I do that?" It's easy, my sister or brother. Just get out of your own way and live from the inside, which is eternal. You can do this, for I have. It was not easy, because I would not get out my own way, so God had no choice but to humble me. This world had affected me, and it grew on me and consumed me and had me thinking I was somebody big, when in actuality I was nothing in this world but a small part of His great plan.

I soon found out after the humbling of my soul and spirit that I really was somebody. I was a child of the King, which made me a prince, and I will later learn to be a king in His Kingdom. You are a king or queen in His courts and your position is awaiting you; your kingdom is all around you and within you, just awaiting your birth and His lordship over your lives, for He is the

King of Kings. It is there for you if you will only believe that there is a better life for you.

Solomon goes on to say that there is a time to weep and a time laugh and also that there is a time to mourn and a time to dance. There is a time to weep, to cry, to feel sad, for your soul has been touched by God Himself. He has given you the power to weep or cry for another, and sometimes for yourself. It is a gift that all of God's creations have. If you listen, really listen, you will hear the Angels weeping for you, the animals crying for one another, and man and woman crying for one another. We weep at funerals when the death of a love one overwhelms us, sometimes because we never told them that we loved them in this life. We weep at marriages, for we know the happiness that is awaiting the newly married couple. Sometimes we weep at graduations, for we know that the individual that's graduating has a little bit of us in them. We know that they have prepared themselves to make it in life, sometimes to go a little farther than we ourselves could go.

Whatever the reason that we weep, it is all good, for weeping brings with it the joy of a better day. I remember a time in my life when I was constantly crying at church, of all places to cry. Being an officer of the church, I had to sit in front of the congregation with my pastor. I was in full view of everyone. There was no hiding my weeping or excusing myself. I often felt shameful and embarrassed and wondered how the people in the congregation were reacting to my emotional display. But I had no control of it, even though I was not burdened about anything or anyone. I would just cry for no reason I knew.

I sought out help because I was concerned. I had a friend, Tonya, who was from Russia doing missionary talks. She informed me that the same thing happened to her quite regularly, and it was nothing to worry about—that God was only cleaning my soul and that the pain and hurt that I had carried all my life was coming out of me. I do know one thing: after I finishing crying, there was usually a release of feeling within my spirit that was indescribable. I couldn't put the feelings to words if I tried.

My weeping usually led into laughter. Everybody needs to laugh, for a life without laughter is a life not lived. There is so much bitterness and disappointment in this measurement of time we call life that we must learn to laugh our way through it, whatever life brings us. Life will bring disappointment, and a lot of it. Laughter is the essence of what makes life great. It is the aroma of pure joy; just like weeping, we laugh at weddings and sometimes at funerals. We laugh and laugh, sometimes so hard that we cry. Laughter is good for the soul.

We understand that laughter is also a release from all fear. When we start laughing about a matter, for some reason we are no longer afraid. We can become fearless and sometimes even feel invincible, for we know that this too shall pass. Whatever was bothering us ceases to hurt us; we have absorbed the pain and hurt.

I believe that laughter is one of the keys to getting through this life untouched by pain, failure, disappointment, misery, heartache, loneliness, and shame. It is just another gift that God gives us to face the seasons of our lives, for there will be times in our lives dominated by darkness in everything that we do. We will ask ourselves where the light is in such a situation. If one learns to laugh through all circumstances and obstacles in life, learns to be patient and silent, then God can speak to you and give the true answer that you truly need. So make a decision to make it to the other side, for your happiness lies on the other side of your sadness; seek it and you will find it. You will live seasons worth living.

Here is a big secret for you. I know that it is hard trying to laugh through life all the time, because our seasons bring more sadness and pain than joy to a good life. But when you learn to laugh within yourself, within your soul, nothing and no one can harm you or take that joy from you, because it resides within your heart, and that is where God lives. And your laughter will turn into gladness.

Solomon shares with us his message on time—there is a time to get and a time to lose, a time to keep and a time to cast away. A time to rend and a time to sew, a time to keep silence and a time to speak. A time to love and a time to hate, a time for war and a time for peace. He says a lot about time. Time and seasons are the same; they both exist on the same plane, and how we handle a time or season is what determines the state of our minds, the completion of our journeys, and the wholeness of our lives. Our God's time is different from our concept of time; His one day is like one thousand years, and compared to our twenty-four-hour day, that is quite a difference. It would also be correct to say that His seasons are different than our seasons and His plans are different than the plans that we follow.

Solomon says that everything that befalls our life has a time, whether it is sowing a seed, keeping silent, or speaking. Whether it is loving one another or it is war or peace, it *will* be, and there *is* a time for it. Time rules and regulates our seasons, thoughts, dreams, plans, and our final destination. Live your seasons well. We might be given the time to carry out all our plans or finish our courses. Or, we might be right in the middle of completing the season when our time runs out.

Time is a precious thing to be respected, and God should be thanked for it. I remember a time in my life after I had just awakened from being in a coma for three days. Even though I had been successful in my business life, even though I was making seven hundred thousand dollars a year, and even though I had a big house complete with a maid to clean it, and even though I had a Mercedes Benz, I had run out of time. I was placed in a coma to fight for my life.

My beloveds, I will tell you that in a coma, there is no such thing as time. There is only space and whiteness. And when I awakened from the coma, all I wanted to do was tell the people that I loved them, which I never did previously, because I was one of those people who thought that I had all the time in the world—that I had three score and ten years promised to me. I tell you now that your time and your seasons go hand in hand. Always respect the time you have remaining, and live your life, for your time is running out, and your seasons are near.

As I write my final words of preaching faith in yourself, hope in your lives, and peace in your seasons, it has begun to snow outside my window. Everything has become completely white. The trees all have a layer of snow upon them, the ground is no longer green, and more flurries are coming from above. Is this not a season? I can remember that a couple of days ago it was summer, and after that it was raining and had become fall, and now it is snowing. Did I make a request that it should snow? Did I request that it should rain? No, I did neither, and nor did I request for the summer to be summer. This is the way that seasons occur in our lives; we have no choice in the matter, and we cannot control the situation or the outcome. We can only live through our seasons day by day, second by second, until the season changes and another starts in our lives.

I am reminded of a story I read in the Bible. There was a young man who had been a great friend of Jesus. His name was Lazarus, and he was greatly loved by Jesus in mutual friendship. The story goes that Lazarus died and had been dead for some days. When Jesus arrived and was told this, He raised his friend from the dead and restored him to this mortal life.

If you look at this story, we realize that Lazarus, his sisters, his family, and even Jesus were all going through seasons in their lives. Lazarus's season was that he had died; his sisters' season was that Jesus had not been there on time when Lazarus had died, his family's season was dealing with all the emotions that death brings on loved ones, and Jesus' season was that his friend, whom he'd loved greatly, had died, and now this family was suffering through the death.

Seasons come to us all. There is no way to go through this life without them occurring. My question is? What effect did this season have upon Lazarus himself? Here was a dead man that had been delivered from death, and was now alive again. He had been awakened from a deep sleep. Did he see the world differently after? Did he see his family differently? I believe he did. He had been where no one had been to and returned. His perspective, concepts, beliefs, and thoughts must all have been changed. Lazarus now had a different view of the world, and his reality was now his existence.

I hope that the short time I have spent with you has awakened you and that you will see life in a new way. I hope that these words will give you greater vitality and a courageous spirit. Mostly, I wish you joyful seasons in your life. I will see you on the other side.

Ronnie V. Broadus

Printed in the United States
by Baker & Taylor Publisher Services